HÔTEL DES ÉTRANGERS

Hôtel
des
Étrangers

POEMS BY
JOACHIM SARTORIUS

German to English
Translation by
Scott J. Thompson

San Francisco, California

ISBN-13: 978-1-7329439-6-4

"Very Green" first appeared in *Four By Two*, Luddite Kingdom Press, Summer 2015; and "Vaucluse, A Solitary Life," "At the Workplace," and "In Writing" appeared in *Toad Suck Review #6*, Department of Writing, University of Central Arkansas, 2016.

Grateful acknowledgement is made to RiskPress Foundation for making The Divers Collection possible.

Cover artwork by Terry St. John

Author photo by Isolde Ohlbaum

fmsbw

San Francisco, California

WE KNOW NOTHING OF LONGING
EXCEPT THAT IT CRYSTALIZES IN IMAGES
AND THAT THESE IMAGES
DO NOT CEASE TO TORMENT US
UNTIL THEY HAVE BEEN MADE REALITY
Octavio Paz

CONTENTS

I. AM ARBEITSPLATZ

I. AT THE WORKPLACE

DIE NACHT VOR DEM PC

Am Schirm halten die blauen Ränder Wunder bereit.
Von Schatten gestützt, beginnt in den Ohren
das Sirren der Sterne am Himmel, welches sagt:

Gib mir alles. Welches ausatmet: Gib mir alles.
Gib mir Erinnerungen, die sich aus der Vergesslichkeit
befreien, Bilder noch im nächtlichen Dunst,

die sich klar wie Mantras ordnen am Tisch.
Wenn alles erblickt ist, werden die Stimmen
süß. *Wir müssen auf Opfer verzichten können.*

Mag der Text weitläufig sein, weit-rillig?,
ein Remix der Platten, die wir bei der Liebe
auflegten, so ist es nicht lächerlich, kein Fehlschlag,

wenn alles jetzt eine Aura hat, blond, illuminert,
hängen geblieben in den Gipfeln des Gedächtnisses.
>>Schau mich an.<< Finger und Finger im Mund,

>>schau mich an<<, die halbe Stadt zu deinen Augen.
Schließ nicht die Augen. Sätze sind so verdreht.
Sie verraten das Flattern des Herzens, die Nässe.

THE NIGHT BEFORE THE COMPUTER

On the screen the blue margins hold wonder in the wings.
Upheld by shadows, the drone of the stars
in the sky begins in the ears, saying;

Give it all to me. Whatever breathes. Give me all of it.
Give me memories that free themselves
from forgetfulness, pictures still veiled in night mist

arranged on the table clear as mantras.
When it's all beheld, the voices turn
sweet. *We must be able to renounce sacrifice.*

If the text 's spun out, worn in the groove?
a remix of the records we stacked up
making love, it's no joke, no blunder

when it's all got an aura these days, blonde, illuminated,
suspended at the peak of recollection.
"Look at me" with fingers finding fingers in mouths.

"Look at me" half the town yours to browse.
Don't close your eyes. Sentences are so distorted.
They betray the fluttering of the heart, the wet spots.

VAUCLUSE, EINSAMES LEBEN
Auf Petrarca

Schwalben über dem Weinlaub
und kleine weiße Wolken schnell ziehend
sehe ich im Fensterrahmen,
wenn ich von den Büchern aufschaue,
und wenn ich den Hals recke,
auch die breite helle Kuppe
des Mont Ventoux, wo ich mich verirrte.

So viel Ruhe hier, in die ich mich
verirre, die ich mir wünschte, lustvoll,
nach dem geschäftigen Avignon.
Der Sonnenstrahl auf meinem Arm ist
so sanft, daß ich Schmerz und Angst vergesse.
Das bloße Licht schafft Leere, die lockt,
Leere und Weite, Empfänglichkeit

für die Vielheit der Welt. Mag sein,
daß ich sündhaft neugierig bin.
Im Buch das Bild eines Fisches.
Ich fange in seinen Augen zu kreisen an
und schmecke das kalte Blut der Kiemen
und sinke und steige – und sehe
Schwalben über dem flirrenden Weinlaub.

Fische schwimmen in der flirrenden Sorgue.
Das Kind meines Gedächtnisses heißt Laura.
Aus gebrochnen Worten spritzt das Licht,
die blonde Locke, das grüne Licht ihres Blicks.
Nie wollte icht, glaubt mir, anderes tun als den Lärm
der Welt mit Worten willkommen zu heißen.
Eine riesige grüne Eiche wird der Abend sein.

VAUCLUSE, SOLITARY LIFE
For Petrarch

Swallows glimpsed over the vine-leaves
and little white clouds flitting past
in the window frame
when I look up from the books,
and when I crane my neck,
the broad bright summit
of Mont Ventoux, too, where I went astray.

So much peace to lose myself in
here, which I longed for, rejoicing,
after that bustling Avignon.
The sunbeam on my arm is
so gentle, that I forget pain and angst.
The naked light begets emptiness, enticing,
emptiness and expanse, receptiveness

for the manifold of the world. May be,
that I am impiously curious.
In the book the plate of a fish.
I begin to revolve in its eyes
and taste the cold blood of the gills
and sink and soar – and see
swallows over the fluttering vine-leaves.

Fish are swimming in the shimmering Sorgue.
The child of my remembrance is called Laura.
The light splashes out of broken words,
 the blonde locks of hair, the green light of her glance.
Never did I want more--believe me—than bid words of welcome
to the noise of the world.
Immensely green the oak turns to evening.

AM ARBEITSPLATZ
Für Hugo Claus

An der Wand neben meinem Schreibtisch
hängt eine römische Dame in Ton.
Sie ist nackt. Rosa Ton. Erstanden
in El Djem (Dorf in der Mitte Tunesiens)
vom Wärter des Kolliseums, rund wie
Rom, weit wie die Hüfte der Dame,
die ihre Arme einladend hebt.
Darunter in der Schrift meines Freundes
Silence, exile & cunning von Joyce.
Nichts hat das miteinander zu tun.
Es ist nur noch einmal an meiner Wand
der Kampf zwischen Vernunft und Gefühl.
Kämpft auch in dir die ratio gegen
das Verlangen, diese römische Dame
zu öffnen, zu erforschen, zu verstehen?
Nichts an ihr ist zu entfernen, denn
sie ist nackt und irden, die Schatten
des Schoßes im Kegel der Lampe scharf,
ein klarer Altar zum Erinnern, und Erinnern.

AT THE WORKPLACE
For Hugo Claus

On the wall next to my desk
hangs a Roman lady in clay.
She is naked. Rose clay. Procured
in the village El-Djem (in the middle of Tunisia)
from the caretaker of the Colliseum, round
like Rome, wide as the lady's hips,
her open arms inviting.
Beneath it in my friend's handwriting
Silence, exile & cunning by Joyce.
Neither one has a thing to do with the other.
There is merely a struggle once more
on my wall between reason and feeling.
Does the ratio in you struggle, too,
against the desire to unlock,
to explore, to understand this Roman lady?
Nothing of hers is left to be undone, for she is
naked and earthen, the shadows of the lap
keen in the taper of the lamp,
a clear altar to remember, and remember.

BEIM SCHREIBEN

Du bist nicht da, mein Tod.

Auf dem Schreibtisch Hefte, Gebetsketten,
Bücher, eine glasierte Kachel aus Samarkand,
ein Notebook, viele kleine dunkle Spiegel.
Die Spiegel, das sind die Worte, zum Spiegeln,
zum Preisen, zum Verletzen, zum Schädelöffnen.
Und da ist Schleifpapier und nach dem Schleifen
Löschpapier, ich weiß nicht ein noch aus.

Das Gedicht versteht mich nicht.

Niemand will eine schnelle Nähe. Das Gedicht
ist ein Traum in Jod. Es gab Wunden.
Die Worte splittern. Der Traum quillt
im papiernen Dickicht hoch, der Schmetterling
ein Gespenst der Raupe. Ich schaue nur zurück,
das Gedicht will nach vorn blicken, will zwei Flügel
haben und verbrennen. Es wartet, dass ich zündele.

Was bringt die Worte zum Leuchten?

Ich nehme die Augenbinde ab. Die Musik
wird lauter. Wo sind deine Augen, wo sind
meine Augen? Ich ordne die Dinge auf dem Tisch.
Die Kerze rußt. Die Spiegel spiegeln nur sich selbst.
Was wissen wir vom Verlangen? Spiegeln auch wir
nur uns selbst? Mein Gesicht im Fensterglas:
Ein von Lamellen schraffierter weißer Schmetterling.

Du bist noch da, mein Tod.

IN WRITING

You are not there, my Death.

On the desk booklets, prayer-beads,
books, a glazed tile from Samarkand,
a notebook, lots of dark little mirrors.
The mirrors; those are the words to reflect on,
to exalt, to wound, to crack open the skull.
And there is sandpaper, and after sanding,
blotting paper at the end of my wits.

The poem does not understand me.

Nobody wants a hasty nearness. The poem
is a dream in iodine. There were wounds.
The words splinter. The dream gushes
to the top in the paper thicket, the butterfly
a ghost of the caterpillar. I merely look back;
the poem wants to look ahead, having two wings
consumed in flame. It waits for me to ignite.

What makes the words luminous?

I take the blindfold off. The music
gets louder. Where are your eyes? Where are
mine? I arrange the things on the table.
The candle smolders. The mirrors reflect only themselves.
What do we know of desire? Is it just our own reflection, too
we gaze at? In the windowpane, my face
hatched from lamina: a white butterfly.

You are still there, my Death.

II. EINIGE BILDGEDICHTE

II. SOME PICTURE POEMS

DAS GEMÄLDE VOM REISKUCHEN

Was Wasser ist, sagt uns der Durst.
Ohne gemalten Hunger wäre der Reiskuchen
nur ein Kuchen. Später, ihn essend, Wasser trinkend,
intonieren wir das unsterbliche Lied vom Sterben.

Aber du wirst auferstehen, singst du,
in dieser Ecke des Bildes, von der Farbe des Reises,
von innen her leuchtend –
und eine Restsüße zieht sich in deinem Gaumen zusammen.

Von der Liebe, die du hattest. Wieder kommen dir
Hände in den Sinn, die vom Hals bis zur Hüfte
liebkosen konnten. Es war still. Es ist still.
Du hörst die Farben, die die Form allein nicht hält.

Eine Linie vom Rund des Kuchens, die rein ist –
und zögernd, da sie vom Leben weiß, vom Durst.
Ein Maler hat ihn gemalt vor 900 Jahren.
Seine Linie führt zu dem Rand, wo Schönheit

Schmerzt (nicht fällt). Jetzt wissen wir,
warum nur manche Dinge Anmut in sich halten können,
und dass – ein solches Bild zu malen – nur möglich ist,
wenn in ihm Liebe ist, vom Bild selbst ausgeschüttet.

THE PAINTING OF THE RICE CAKE

Thirst teaches us what water is.
Without painted hunger the rice cake would be
just a cake. Later, eating it, drinking water,
we intone the undying Song of the Dying.

But you will arise, you sing,
in this corner of the picture, of the color of the rice,
lustre glowing forth from within –
and a remaining sweetness mashes together in your
    palate.

Of the love you once had. Hands again
cross your mind that from neck to hips
could caress. It was still. It is still.
You hear the colors the form alone does not contain.

Round the orb of the cake, a line that is pure
and wavering, as it knows of life, of thirst.
A painter painted it 900 years ago.
His line draws to the edge, where beauty

aches (not falls). Now we know
why only some things can in themselves contain grace
and that – to paint such a picture – is only possible,
if there is love in it, overflowing from the picture itself.

PAN UND SYRINX
Peter Paul Rubens zu Jan Brueghel d. Ä.

Du stellst die Landschaft und die Tiere dar,
ich die Personen, den geilen Pan und Syrinx,
die Scheue im Schilf. Die einzelnen Halme –
da bist du der Meister, auch Frösche, Vögel,
das rettende Wasser. Wenn Pan statt der Nymphe
Schilf in den Armen hält, da bist du gefragt,
sollst du es malen. Teamwork ist gut. Es geht
schneller von der Hand, schnell zum Käufer.
Auch mein Pan will schnell zum Ziel, greift
mit der Hand das Tuch, das kaum noch sie verhüllt,
mit dem Arm das Schilfbündel, als sei Verwandlung
schon im Gange. Warum ist Syrinx so verhalten?
Er ist ganz Drängen, und dein Frosch stiebt davon.
Brauner Tierkörper. Schimmerndes Inkarnat.
Nervös nimmt mein Pinsel die Verfolgung auf.
Müssen wir sie uns als schon verwandelt denken?
Pan schnitzt aus ihr, aus diesem Schilf die Flöte.
Nicht von allen wird seine Musik verstanden.
Doch ist sie einfach: Erinnerung an die verlorene,
nie besessene Frau. Überhaupt, Jan, findet sich
in deiner üppigen Landschaft viel zu viel Schilf.

PAN AND SYRINX

Peter Paul Rubens to Jan Brueghel, the Elder

You depict the landscape and the animals,
I, the persons, the lusty Pan and Syrinx,
the coyness in the reeds. The individual blades –
there, you are the master, also frogs, birds,
the rescuing water. If instead of the nymph, Pan
holds reeds in his arms, then it is you in demand;
you should paint it. Teamwork is good. It speeds
through our hands, hastening to the buyer.
My Pan, too, will speed to the goal, seizing
hold of the garment that just barely veils her,
the bundle of reeds in his arms, as if transformation
were already underway. Why is Syrinx so restrained?
He is all impulse, and your frog flees from it.
Brown body of a beast. Glistening flesh-tone.
Nervously my paintbrush takes up the pursuit.
Must we imagine her to ourselves as if already transformed?
Out of her, out of these reeds, Pan whittles the flute.
Not everyone will understand his music.
Yet it is simple: Remembrance of the lost woman
never possessed. Overall, Jan, one finds
in your voluptuous landscape far too many reeds.

EIN KORB GLÄSER (1644)
Von Sebastian Stoskopff

Sind das, unordentlich aufgehäuft,
die Gläser nach dem Abwasch?
Nie gehen wir so mit Gläsern um.
Lichtreflexe als Ordnungsprinzip.

Jahrzehnte muß dieser arme Maler
dem Studium der Wiedergabe
von Transparenz geopfert haben,
und ja, von Licht und Dunkel

und, ja, mit Mengen Branntwein.
Brillant sind die Gläser, makellos rein,
ein abrupter Verlust jederzeit möglich.
Nah am Tischrand Scherben.

So funkelnd hat der Trunkenbold
diese Scherben gemalt, schöner
als die heilen Gläser im Korb.
Zu deutlich ist das.

Dünn wie ein Hauch sind die Gläser.
Schwerelos, fluchtige Erscheinung,
künden sie von einer anderen,
einer geläuterten Existenz.

Keiner seiner Kollegen in Frankreich
hat das geschafft, diese Darstellungen
von Glas, diese Stille, diesen Verlust
in Scherben, diesen hellen Triumph.

STILL LIFE WITH BASKET OF GLASSES (1644)
By Sebastian Stoskopff

Are those the glasses
stacked up carelessly after dishwashing?
Never do we deal with glasses that way.
Light reflection as arranging principle.

Decades this poor painter
must have sacrificed to the study
of reproducing transparency
and, yes, of light and dark

and, yes, with plenty of brandy.
The glasses are brilliant, flawlessly pure,
An abrupt loss possible at any moment.
Broken fragments near the edge of the table.

Sparkling so, these fragments
the drunkard painted more beautiful
than the undamaged glasses in the basket.
It is all too clear.

The glasses are thin as a breath.
Weightless, ephemeral apparition,
bearing witness of another,
of a chastened existence.

No other colleague of his in France
has achieved that, these depictions
of glass, this stillness, this loss
in fragments, this shining triumph.

JUDITH VOR DER RESTAURIERUNG
Für Andrea

Dieses Bild aus dem Barock
von einem schlechten, unbekannnten Maler
ist ein Wrack, die Farbe in kleinen Schollen
lose vom Bildträger hängend.
Mit geöffnetem Craquelé
im Dekolleté
reißt Judiths gelbe Haut
an den Spannrändern auf,
Ein komplexes Schadensbild
von den Launen der Zeit.

Holofernes, braunhaarig, nur Haupt noch,
verschlossen, ist nicht zu retten, aber
Judith braucht dringend Hilfe,
Salzlösungen im Klimazelt,
Ein Bad mit Wasserleim
Und delikateste Pinsel,
geführt von fühlsamer Hand.
Die Perlen in ihrem Haar
könnten wieder leuchten
und Augenlider neu erfunden werden.

JUDITH BEFORE THE RESTORATION
For Andrea

This picture from the Baroque
by a bad, unknown painter
is a wreck, the colors in little flakes
hanging loose from the stretcher.
With opened craquelure
in the decolleté
Judith's yellow skin
rips open at the stretched border,
a complex picture of abrasion
from the tempers of the time.

Holofernes, brown-haired, still just head,
withdrawn, is not to be rescued, but
Judith needs urgent help,
alkaline solutions in the climate-control tent
a bath with aqueous adhesives
and the most delicate paintbrush,
guided by a more sentient hand.
The pearls in her hair
could be glossy again
and eyelids be made up anew.

LIEBESPAAR (ca. 1870)
Von Hashimoto Chikanobu

Er zupft an ihrer Minze.
Sie trägt einen Komono, blaugrau gemustert,
darunter ein rotes Gewand (grell rot),
das um ihren weißen Bauch eine zweite Vulva legt.

Vom Liebespaar
sehen wir: Ihr verzücktes Gesicht,
sein verzücktes Gesicht, keine Brüste,
keinen Phallus, keine Schenkel.

Alles ist Rascheln des Gewandes.
Muster der Stoffe, rot, rot, und blau, und grau.
Wie lange hat Chikanobu das untersucht?
Wie Körper unter Stoffen sich darstellen lassen?

Alles ist verborgen, außer dem Geheimsten.
Ihre Scheide, der Ursprung der Welt.
Kleine Lippen, aufgebogen unter der Minze,
und die sinnlichste Kurve der Welt.

LOVING PAIR (ca. 1870)
By Hashimoto Chikanobu

He tugs at her pubic hair.
She wears a kimono, blue-gray patterned,
underneath it a red gown (glaring red)
round her white belly, pleating a second vulva.

Of the Loving Pair
we see: her rapt face,
his rapt face, no breasts,
no phallus, no thigh.

Everything is a rustling of the gown.
Pattern of the material, red, red, and blue, and gray.
How long did Chikanobu investigate that?
How bodies represent themselves under fabric?

Everything is under wraps, apart from the most secret.
Her sheath, the origin of the world.
Little lips, unfolding under the pubic hair,
the most sensuous curve of the world.

MARIONETTEN AM MEER
An Marwan und Soutine denkend

Doch küßten wir uns oft mit Armen,
Fackelschlägen, und tranken auf die Wut,

sich verbeißende Augen, Fischgebell,
den Rückzug an blauer Nylonschnur.

>>Die Moränen sind da.<< Feuchte
Gehirnbäume mit undeutlichem Ende.

>>Die Vögel sind da.<< Der Morgenstern.
Und Regen nach der Regenzeit.

Der Atem ruckt am Rückgrat.

Tintenfische zischen am Haken

und zählen im Sterben ihre Näpfe,
drücken Tinte ab in deine reichen Augen.

MARIONETTES ASHORE

Thinking of Marwan and Soutine

But we often kissed each other with arms,
blows of the torch, and drank to rage,

to locked eyes, to the yelp of fishes,
their retreat on blue nylon string.

"The moraines are here." Moist
treelike brains with fuzzy endings.

"The birds are here." The morning star.
And rain after the rainy season.

The breath draws on the backbone.
Squids sizzle on the hook

and count their suckers in dying,
squirting ink in your rich eyes.

ANTLITZ
Für Marwan

Die Stille reift
wie Steine eine Rinde bilden
der Stoff darunter vom gleichen Stoff
bis zum Grud ändert sich nichts
umsonst hackt der Blick auf Raum auf Zeit
überall ist das Gesicht offen da

Die Löcher in dem Gesicht
sind Brunnen aus denen die Stille steigt
Erinnerungen aus Silben und Vornamen

So ist der Kopf aus Schrift
Auch die Schrift bildet eine Haut
Das Fleisch darunter auch aus Schrift
Manchmal fließt ein Gesicht in ein anderes
Pinselstriche sind Kürzel für das Leben
Sie bannen den Tod weil sie ihn üben

Dieses Gesicht ist eine Welt
denn es gibt nur das Gesicht
gebaut und verworfen und
wieder errichtet vibrierend
vom Tod in das Leben
und zurück plötzlich Antlitz
unauslöschbar

Kein Unterschied mehr
zwischen Spiegel und Glas
und zurückgegebenem Blick
mein Blick
will dieses Antlitz sein

VISAGE
For Marwan

The stillness ages
like stones forming a crust
the matter underneath of the same stuff
no variation at all right to the core
in vain the gaze hacks at space at time
everywhere the face there is open

The holes in the face
are fountains the stillness rushes from
Memories made of syllables and first names

Thus is the head fashioned from script
The script also forming a skin
The flesh underneath from script as well
Sometimes one face flows into another
Brush strokes are contractions for life
They banish death because they put it to use

This face is a world
For there is only the face
constructed and thrown away and
erected again vibrating
of death in life
and suddenly back to visage
inextinguishable

No more difference
between mirror and glass
and reflected glance
my glance
wants to be this visage

IN AN OLD BOOK
Radierung von David Hockney (1966)

Diese Sonne dieses Licht auf den Laken
wie es die Augenlider wegbrennt
auf den Laken der Marmorleib
wie von jenen Statuen
ohne Makel ohne Makel ohne Makel
keine Spur von den Zähnen des Freundes
von seinen spitzen Rippen
nur Zärtlichkeiten von einer kleinen Insel zur
    nächsten
alles was sie tun
macht sie benommen
und schläfrig und durstig

Im Traum kehren sie die Schaben
die Dornen die toten Blätter unter das Bett
das Geröll unter das Meer

IN AN OLD BOOK
Etching by David Hockney (1966)

This sun this light on the sheets
as it burns away the eyelids
on the sheets the marble body
as of those statues
without blemish without blemish without blemish
no trace of the teeth of the friend
of his sharp ribs
only tenderness from one little isle to the
    next
all that they do
makes them bewildered
and sleepy and thirsty

In the dream they turn the cockroaches
the thorns the dead leaves under the bed
the rubble under the sea

CÄSARION

In die Mitte
des Brauns
des Abhangs des Halses
stößt die Schlange zu
im Biß springt die Gemme
aus dem Ring
rollt
zwischen die eisernen Knie
des Cäsars ins straffe Laken

wie geht es weiter,
fragt sie und start in die leere Höhle
des Rings, das Sehen tief
schon ins Auge gescharrt,
das Gesicht voll Verweigerung schon,
schöner, schöner
als im Leben,
das gerade von ihr geht –

und ihr Sohn, von Cäsar,
den sie in der Hocke gabar,
ein Kind ohne Zukunft,
liebkost den schimmernden Knieschutz,

die wie Schwertklingen zugespitzten Schienbeine,
gedengelt von Hieben der (Tod)feinde,
plötzlich unansehnlich:
aufgeschmolzen.

CAESARION

In the middle
of the brown
of the slope of the neck
the snake thrusts
in the bite the gem pops
out of the ring
rolling
between the iron knees
of Caesar into the taut sheets

how does it go on,
she asks and stares into the empty hollow
of the ring, the vision
already deeply scratched into the eye,
face already full of refusal,
lovelier, lovelier
than in life
that is just departing her –

and her son, from Caesar,
whom she bore squatting,
a child without a future,
caresses the shimmering knee guard,

the shin bones pointed like sword blades,
hammered by blows of the (mortal) foe,
suddenly unseemly:
molten.

DER MALER, DIE SCHÖNHEIT
Auf Joachim Patinir

I. Le balcon du monde

Der heilige Patinir
endeckte für die Malerei
die unendliche Welt.
Hundert Flüsse fließen
zum Horizont, der sich krümmt.
Die Seelchen sind klein
in der Landschaft der Welt.
Sie flattern in der Herrlichkeit der Welt.
Flügellos fliegen sie und
doch in Licht, in Luft,
in leerem, kaltem, glanzvollem Blau.

Die Pilgerschaft ist lustvoll:
Gegabelte Wege zuhauf.
Irrtümer zuhauf.
Daß wir, alles im Blick,
über die Erde fliegen können,
die sichtbare Welt ein Balkon,
unermeßlich reich für die Sinne,
daß aber die richtige, wirkliche Welt
hinter dem Horizont liegt
und dort ungeduldig auf uns wartet.

II.

Das Blau is so wild, so heftig,
als habe der Maler ein Gedicht
auf Glas gekratzt: Ein Gedicht
von der Natur, die Gott ist,

THE PAINTER, THE BEAUTY
To Joachim Patinir

I. Le balcon du monde

The holy Patinir
discovered for painting
the never-ending world.
Hundreds of rivers flowing
towards the bending horizon.
The soulkins are small
in the landscape of the world.
In its splendor they flutter,
flying wingless and
yet in light, in air
in empty, cold, glorious blue.

The pilgrimage is full of delight:
Forked roads abound.
Errors abound.
That we, gazing at it all,
may fly above the earth,
the visible world a balcony,
immeasurably rich for the senses,
but that the correct, actual world
lies behind the horizon,
waiting impatiently for us there.

II.

The blue is so wild, so violent,
as though the painter had scratched
a poem into glass: a poem
of the nature that God is,

so unendlich, daß der, der schaut,
selbst blau und tief
und Zeuge wird,
wie sich das Blau aufgibt,

weiter draußen, und auch
er sich aufgibt, nur noch
Widerschein des Lichts von drüben,
vom glatten leeren Flur Gottes.

III.

Ohne Umschweife
klettern die Augen
an Birnen vorbei
an gelben Vögeln
die Bäume hinauf
ins Lichtgefüge
und weiten das Herz.

IV. Die Schönheit der Felsen

Ist es Abbild
oder nur harter Schwamm,
der alle Weite in sich gesogen hat?
Manche sagen, die Felsen
hätten Gesichter. Ich sehe
sie nicht. Die Felsen sind
Felsen, die Engel sind Engel.

Das Blau ist blau.

Und Charon steuert
nach rechts schon
dummes Seelchen!
Hinter der Lieblichen Mündung
lauert der Cerberus. Er hat
drei böse Gesichter. Dann
beginnen Felsen und Feuer.

so unending, that whoever looks
becomes blue and deep himself,
witness to
how the blue leaves off,

further out, and he leaves
himself too, mere
reflection of light from the other side,
from the polished empty hallway of God.

III.

In a beeline
the eyes ascend
over pears
past yellow birds
up the trees
into the scaffold of light,
expanding the heart.

IV. The Beauty of the Rocks

Is it likeness
or just sponge without pity
that's sucked all immensity into itself?
The rocks have faces,
many say. I do not
see them. The rocks are
rocks, the angels are angels.

The blue is blue.

And Charon's already
rowing starboard,
dumb soulkin!
Behind the charming inlet
lurks Cerberus. He has
three evil faces. Then
begins fire and brimstone.

V. Gestürzte Idole

Zwei goldene Füße auf einer Steinkugel.
Die Beine abgerissen
kurz über dem Knöchel.
Wo ist der Rest, der große Götze?
Verjagt, erhängt.

Weiter links, in Heliopolis,
fliegen goldene Idole
vom Tempeldach,
während der Rattengott
noch Opfer kaut.

Die Pilgerschaft ist eine Wanderung
zwischen dem Guten und dem Bösen.

VI. Brennen und gehen

Mit Engeln an den Händen
horchen Lot und seine Töchter
nur noch in sich hinein.
Der weiße Strich
exakt in der Mitte des Bildes:
Lots Frau, eine Salzsäule,
erbärmlich, winzig.

Die Feuerzungen nicht auszumachen.
Ihre Zahl? Hundert und mehr.
Das Lid schlägt, schlägt und schlägt.
Da, wo die Rehe waren, wird es bald
hart glänzen, unter dem Knochenzelt.
Die Landschaft verfriert in der Glut.

V. Fallen Idols

Two golden feet on a ball of stone.
The legs broken off
just above the ankle.
Where is the rest, the great pagan idol?
Banished, hanged.
Further left, in Heliopolis,
golden idols are flying
from the roof of the temple
while the God of the Rats
still gnaws on sacrifices.

The pilgrimage is a wandering
between the good and the evil.

VI. Burning and leaving

With angels by the hand
Lot and his daughters hearken
only within themselves.
The white line
exactly in the middle of the painting:
Lot's wife, a pillar of salt,
pitiful, tiny.

The fiery tongues not to be extinguished.
Their number? Hundreds and more.
The lid pounding, pounding, pounding.
There, where the deer were, it will soon
flash without mercy, under the bone vault.
The landscape is frozen in the glow.

VII. Fluß, Fließen, Strom, Strömung

Die Gletscherzungen ziehen sich zurück
die erhitzten Eiskapen strömen dahin
die Lippen rutschen
zum Schlitz der Welt

das Seelchen weiß nicht ein nicht aus
nicht Schritt mit dem Verlangen halten
können seine Augen

Buchten öffnen den Blick
auf geöffnete Buchten
das Licht gefiltert
durch blaue fließende Gehäuse

Was hat mich gefroren fragt
der Maler ein Wunderer denn
wäscht die Schönheit nicht die Toten

VIII. (Der bläuliche Patinir)

für Milos Sovak

Azur, blau, blaue Lasuren

für ihn, diesen bläulichen Patinir,
waren der Eremit, die Anbetung,
Maria auf der Flucht nach Ägypten
                nichts
als Requisiten einer anderen Sehnsucht

einer Sehnsucht in Träumen
surrealer Landschaften, in den Sinnen, nein,
über den Sinnen, nein, im blauen Wasser
um die Knie des Täufers (Beiwerk),
nein, über dem Wasser,
                auf dem Horizont

VII. Flux, Flowing, Stream, Streaming

The glacier tongues draw themselves back
the heated icecaps stream forth
the lips slide
to the crack of the world

the soulkin not knowing where to turn
His eyes cannot keep pace
With his longing

Bays open the view
upon opened bays
the light filtered
through blue flowing cubes

What has frozen me asks
the painter, for a marveler
washes the beauty not the dead

VIII. (The bluish Patinir)

for Milos Sovak

Azure, blue, blue ultramarines

for him, this bluish Patinir,
the hermit, the adoration,
Maria on the flight to Egypt
            were nothing
but requisites of another longing

of a longing in dreams
surreal landscapes, in the senses, no
above the senses, no, in the blue water,
at the knee of the baptist (frills),
no, above the water,
            on the horizon.

Patinir, deine Sehnsucht spannte sich
                    über die Haut der Augen,
Sie dehnte sich
                    zum Himmel für die Malerei

Patinir! Patinir!

dein massives Blau, weißes Blau
nichts

                    verstehen wir mehr
Illusion und Gegenstand
diese verflügelten Bilder
Anmut und Azur
wohltuende
                    Panik

Patinir, your longing stretches
          over the film of the eye,
extending itself
          for painting to the heavens

Patinir! Patinir!

your massive blue, white blue
nothing
          do we understand more
illusion and object
these pictures on the wing
grace and azure
exquisite
          panic

III. STÄDTE DES OSTENS

III. CITIES OF THE EAST

ODESSA, BEI BETRACHTEN EINER KARTE
DES SCHWARZEN MEERES
Für Rebecca Horn

Hier ist graugrün
das Asowsche Meer,
Bild von trostlosen Steppen,
auf denen die Barbaren alles hinwegfegten,
Griechen, Römer, Skythen, Sarmaten.
Kleine Vierecke, viele sinds,
zeigen die Gräber,
tief in di Erde gebetterte Prinzessinnen
mit dem Zaumzeug von 49 Pferden
und jeder Menge Diadem.
Nur die Fingerknöchel
weggenagt
von Mäusen.

Hier hochbraun der Kaukasus, auch Schnee,
weiße Schlieren mit dünnem blauen Rand,
aber die Küste hellgrün von Bananenblättern,
helles Suchumi, Batumi,
und fröhlich eingestrichelt
die hüpfenden Tümmler,
Und weiter rechts siehst du die Ströme
– Don, Dnjepr, Kuban –
ihre Mündungen
mit braunen sich verweigenden Netzen,
die Laichgründe, die Schelfs.

Und die Schiffe, weiß und regelmäßig,
stampfend zur türkischen Grenze
bis nach Trabzon und Sinop,
deren Silbermünzen
die Göttin zeigten
(mit prahlerischem Ohrgehänge)
und den glatten Delphin.

ODESSA, UPON GAZING AT A MAP
OF THE BLACK SEA

For Rebecca Horn

The Sea of Azov
here is grey-green,
vista of desolate steppes,
where barbarians swept all away,
Greeks, Romans, Scythians, Sarmatians.
Little squares, lots of them,
designate the graves
of princesses reposing deep in the earth
with the bridle gear of 49 horses
and heaps of diadems.
Only their knuckles
gnawed away
by mice.

The Caucasus here, deep brown, snow as well,
white striae with thin blue border,
but the coast, bright green from banana leaves,
bright Sukhumi, Batumi,
and the hopping tumbler
sketched in with a flair.
And further right you see the rivers
-Don, Dnieper, Kuban-
their estuaries
branching out with brown nets,
the spawning grounds, the shelves.

And the ships, white and regular,
tramping the Turkish border
as far as Trebizond and Sinope,
whose silver coins
displayed the Goddess
(with gaudy earrings)
and sleek dolphins.

Die Linien der Schiffahrt
sind hellblau
und laufen alle, fast alle,
leicht gebogen wie zu einem Blütenkelch
auf Odessa zu,
den roten Punkt
im Lampenruß der Uferstraße.

Was kann Heimat für Odessa sein?
Nicht dein Blick, nicht dieses Bild.
Es mag der verlorene Brief von Isaak Babel sein,
voller Vorwürfe, an Ovid.
Daß er in Tomis über Rom
und nicht über Tomis geschrieben hat.
Vielleicht ist dieses Selbstmitleid der Städte
Heimat. Daß die großen Zeiten vorbei sind.
Die Treppe nicht mehr so groß,
der Fährenterminal kaput.
Aber das Schwarze Meer kannst du
nur schildern
mit deinem Alphabet.

Das schwarze Meer? Auf der Karte
ein sanftes blaues Oval,
in welches die Krim eine dicke, seltsame
braune Troddel hängt. Was wußten
die Kartographen von der Hitze der Geschichte?
Daß die Barbaren die früheren Völker
einschmolzen in die Risse der anderen?
Waren den Zeichnern die früheren Städte
    bewußt,
Olbia zum Beispiel, das reich wurde
mit Weizen, Trockenfisch und Sklaven?
Unermeßlich Schönes schufen ihre Künstler.
In den Vitrinen des Provinzmuseums
erleben wir es wie einen Umsturz im Kopf.

The lines of navigation
are light blue,
and they all taper, almost all,
lightly curved like a calyx
to Odessa,
the red point
in the lamp-soot of the shore road.

What can home for Odessa be?
Not your glance, not this picture.
It may be Isaac Babel's lost letter
to Ovid, full of reproach
that in Tomis he wrote
about Rome and not about Tomis.
Perhaps this self-pity of the cities
is home. That the great times are past.
The steps not so great any more,
the ferry terminal *kaputt.*
But the Black Sea
you can only depict
with your alphabet.

The Black Sea? On the map
a soft blue oval,
where a brown tassel of the Crimea
is suspended thick and strange.
What did cartographers know
of the heat of history?
That the barbarians melted the earlier people
down into the rifts of the others?
Were the earlier cities known
  to the draftsmen,
Olbia for example, that grew rich
in wheat, dried fish and slaves?
Immeasurable the beauty their artists created.
In the display cases of the provincial museums
we experience it like an upheaval in the head.

Odessa sollte Odessos heißen.
Eine Laune von Katharina der Großen,
eine weibliche Stadt. Wie viele
hat sie in ihre Pflaume gesteckt?
Was ist die Schönheit dieser Stadt?
Ihre Anlage? Ihre Frauen? Ihr Licht?
Vom Verfall zu wissen.
Alles kann verfallen.
Paläste, Körper, Säulen.

Aber Odessa kannst du
nur schildern
mit deinem Alphabet.

Ganz oben auf der Treppe steht: Urania.
Sie wäscht die Stadt in Azur,
rollt den Morgen heran.
Ein glanzperlenheißer Schauer
über den Steinen des Hafens,
dem Beton, den Mollusken, dem Meer.
Urania drischt auf Glas (Glas des Geistes),
Kristallnetze,
vom goldenen Stab bewegt.
Und mitten ins hellblaue Kartenwasser gesetzt
die Kompaßrose,
ihr Unterströmen und Entfalten,
so mit sich im Kreis verwindet,
daß jeder Perle beigesellt ist
der große Kreis des Universums.

So breitet sich Odessa aus
von der obersten Stiege der Treppe,
großes Geviert, von Bäumen durchquert,
über Schluchten, die zu den Schifen springen –
schönes genaues Spielbrett,
spielerisch vom Wasser hochgehoben,
den Gezeiten ausgessetzt,
im Nadir der Mond.

Odessa should be called Odessos.
A mood of Catherine the Great,
a feminine city. How many
has she tucked into her plum?
What is the beauty of this city?
Her arrangement? Her women? Her light?
To know of ruin.
Everything can fall into ruin.
Palaces, bodies, pillars.

But Odessa
you can only depict
with your alphabet.

At the very top of the stairs stands: Urania.
She bathes the city in azur,
rolls the morning on.
A sparkling pearly hot shower
over the stones of the harbor,
the concrete, the mollusks, the sea.
Urania threshes out of glass (glass of the spirit),
crystal nets
touched by the golden staff.
And planted in the middle of the bright blue charted water
the compass rose,
her undercurrents and unveiling,
so poised within herself in the circle,
that every pearl is joined together
in the great circle of the universe.

Thus does Odessa display herself
from the upper staircase of the steps,
great quadrat, traversed by trees,
over ravines, that plunge to the ships –
graceful faultless game board,
the tides playfully suspended
by the high water heaving
in the nadir, the Moon.

Die Odessiter sammeln sich um Urania.
An ihrem Zeigestab entlang
blicken sie auf den Hafen,
die Schiffsstraßen zwischen den Kränen
vor der schwarzen Einfahrt.
Und hier, an Land, überall Katzen,
die ihre engen roten Kiefer lecken
unter dem großen Gewicht der Zeit.
Was ist die Schönheit dieser Stadt?
Sie ist so schön wie alle meine Geheimnisse.
Die Nacht springt aus dem Fenster
von Platane zu Akazie, von einer Grille
zum Mond, vom Voroncov-Palais
zum dunklen Riesenspiegel darunter.

Aber auf der Karte ist das Meer
stets von hellem Blau und in der Tiefe
leblos und tot.
Wir fühlen
nur dem Salz nach,
das durch unsere Träume trieb.
Nur dem Glimmen der Störe,
wo kein Grund mehr sichtbar ist.

The Odessians assemble themselves around Urania.
Along their indicator
they look out on the harbor,
the shipping lanes between the cranes
ahead of the black entrance.
And here on land, cats everywhere,
licking their slender red chops
under the immense burden of time.
What is the beauty of this city?
She is as beautiful as all of my secrets.
The night springs out of the window
from the plane trees to acacias, from a cricket
to the moon, from the Vorontsov palace
to the dark gigantic looking-glass below.

But on the map the sea
is always of bright blue and in the depths
lifeless and dead.
We feel
only the salt afterwards,
that drifted through our dreams.
Only the glimmer of the sturgeons
where the bottom can be seen no more.

TUNIS 1957

Da ist in dem Plastikalbum >>Sommer<<
ein verblassendes Foto und darauf
bin ich im Leeren, schräg
zwischen Himmel und Meer, und neben mir,
eingeklebt, ein Stadtplan von Tunis,
auf dem sich alles vermischt,
die Korantafeln und die Davidsterne,
die Klage von Oum Kalsum und das Lied von Ferid
al Atrache,
das Lächeln dunkler Frauen und mindestens
45° im Schatten meines Herzens, und vor der Stadt
die Düne von Gammarth, das klebrige Moos auf den
Felsen.
Und die Palmen und die Frische? Die Lippen (Psalmen)
und die Augen (Fische) schlugen vor Verlangen.
Ferne ist eine Lüge. Auch Zeit ist eine Lüge,
der Himmel eine Farbe (blau), und alles nah
wie ein Stachel:

Das Geräusch des siedenden Öls. Die *beignets*,
in einen Zeitungsfetzen gewickelt: >>Attention,
tres chaud!<< mit Blick auf den Golf.
Ich wollte immer pünktlich sein,
am glücklichen Augenblick.

TUNIS 1957

In the plastic album "Summer"
there's a faded photo, and there
I am in the emptiness, oblique
between sky and sea, and beside me,
pasted in, is a city map of Tunis,
on which everything's jumbled together,
the plates of the Koran and the Star of David,
the lament of Umm Kulthum and the song of Farid
al-Atrash,
the smile of sultry women, and at least
45° in the shade of my heart, and before the city
the sand dunes of Gammarth, the clinging moss
            on the rocks.
And the palms and the freshness? The lips (psalms)
and the eyes (fishes) throbbed with longing.
Distance is a lie. And time's a lie;
the sky a color (blue), and everything's close
as an urchin's spine:

The sound of the simmering oil. The *beignets*
wrapped in scraps of newspaper: "*Attention,
tres chaud*!" with glance at the Gulf.
I always wanted to be on the dot
at the lucky moment.

DIE VÖGEL VON SFAX

Nicht ein Schlafbaum. Alle Bäume der Stadt
sind ihre Schlafbäume. Ihr Zwitschern
ist voll Begeisterung, ansteckend
wie das Zwitschern der Sterne dort oben.
Die Kasbah leuchtet. Die Peitschenlampen leuchten.
Der betäubende Gesang reißt nicht ab:
Kommt her, kommt her, es gibt noch einen Platz.
Tschilpen bis zum Anschlag, zum Tod.

Das Zimmer, der Vorhang, die Welt wird Schwarz.
Geschlossene Jalousien. Die Augen schieben sich
in die Spalten, und dann vergessen wir den ganzen Lärm
in den Bäumen. Die Stadt wird größer.
Es gibt den Platz für die Toten und den Platz
für den Himmel. Das singen,
von Sommer zu Sommer, die Stare.

THE BIRDS OF SFAX

Not one tree to sleep in. All the trees in town
are their sleeper trees. Their twittering
is replete with inspiration, contagious
like the twittering of the stars there above.
The kasbah twinkles. Whip-shaped lamps sparkle.
The deafening singing does not cease:
come 'ere, come 'ere, there's still a place.
Chirping to the point of assault, to the death.

The room, the curtain, the world grows black.
Venetian blinds are shut. Eyes shift
into the cracks, and then we forget all the noise
in the trees. The city gets bigger.
There's the place for the dead and the place
for the sky. From summer to summer
that's what the starlings sing.

KERKENNAH

Vielleicht sind die Inseln, die man nie sieht,
die besten, geschützt, fern, ein Name bloß,
schwer auszumachen dann, wo du bist und
wo ich bin, und welche Hirne uns verdecken.

Das Geräusch der Eiswürfel im Glas, wo die Nacht
endet, im Bett mit Frau Morse. Heure Bleue.
Das Herz raschelt frisch wie Basilikum.
Der Videoschirm granatapfelkernfarben.

Das Land ist flach, die Palmen räudig.
Kein Wind, nur die sich in ihrem Kummer
wiegenden Bäume. Ich grabe am Meer
Statuen aus. Die Stimme des Wärters dröhnt.

Oft macht einem ein Traum Angst
vor den Dingen, die man tun könnte.
Hinter dem Tempel stolpere ich
über die zerfallenen Körper eines jungen Paars.

KERKENNAH

Perhaps the islands one never sees are
the best ones, sheltered, far off, merely a name.
For it's hard to make out, where you are and
I am, and which brains hide us from view.

The clink of ice-cubes in the glass, where the night
ends, in bed with Ms. Morse, Heure Bleue.
The heart murmurs fresh as basil.
The videoscreen the color of pomegranate seeds.

The land is flat, the palm trees shabby.
No wind. Just the trees swaying their trunks
in dismay. I exhume statues
on the seashore. Loud voice, that watchman.

Often a dream makes you anxious,
Faced with the things you could do.
Behind the temple I stumble
over a young couple's bodies in ruins.

FISCHITANI, RABAT?
Für Mohammed Bennis

Gibt es noch was anderes, Rabat,
als dein blasses Marzipan, deine antiken
    Wasserverkäufer,
das Mädchen am Straßenrand, das den Passanten
auf Sufi anspricht (>>Willst du mein Rautenherz
durchblättern?<<), als deine Schrift,
die ich nicht nur liebe, weil ich sie nicht verstehe?

Was anderes als die orangene Katze
vor der güldenen Auslage des Juweliers? Oder
ist sie neben dem Wesen das höhere Wesen,
welches das Blatt der Zunge öffnet und raunt?
Vom farblosen Vogel mit den leuchtenden Flügeln?
Von ihrem Öffnen und Schließen und Öffnen?

Wie Deserteure finden wir geräumige Stille
bei dir, drinken unter der Palme zwei süße Tees.
Begeistern uns für Massage und Schlamm, Lack, Liebe,
überhitzte Mineralien, einen belebenden Abrieb.
Dann – als könnte es gebraucht werden, als sei es
für die Kunst – stecke ich ein Körnchen Zweifel

in dein großporiges Herz, und beobachte,
wie alles, was klein war, sich ausdehnt
und alles andere verdampft.
Endlich wissen wir:
Der schöne Augenblick ist unvergänglich.
Gewaschene Seide gestillten Dursts.

FISHITANI, RABAT?

For Mohammed Bennis

Is there still something else, Rabat,
besides your pallid marzipan, your antique
  water vendors,
the girl at the curb, accosting
passers-by in Sufi ("Want to thumb through
my diamond heart?"), besides your script
that I don't just love because I can't understand it?

What else besides the orange cat
before the jeweller's golden showcase? Or
is she the higher being next to the creature,
opening the blade of her tongue and murmuring?
Of the pale bird with brilliant wings?
Of their spreading open and closing and spreading open?

Like deserters we find a roomful of silence
by your side, drinking two sweet teas under palms.
We delight in massage and mud, lacquer, love,
overheated minerals, an invigorating rub down.
Then--as though it could be used, as though it were
for art-- I plant a grain of doubt

in your porous heart, and observe
how everything that was small stretches out
and everything else evaporates.
In the end we know:
the beautiful moment's imperishable.
Bathed silk of quenched thirst.

SEHR GRÜN

Es gibt einen Gott dort, in Damaskus,
in einem großen Museum
in einer kleinen Vitrine
einen sehr grünen Gott.
Vor 3400 Jahren war er nicht vergeßlich
und brach nie seine Versprechen.
Jetzt wirft er einen amüsierten Blick auf Touristen.
Die Goldschicht, die übrig geblieben ist,
hindert ihn, die Arme zu verschränken.
Eine Hand ist immer zum Gruß erhoben,
die andere hält etwas, das verschwand.

Am Rand der Stadt
gibt es eine sehr grüne Kuppel.
Unter ihr liegt Ibn el-Arabi
in seinem Schrein. Unter dieser Kuppel,
unter dem breiten Gewölbe
eines schwarzgrünen Turbans
liegt er, der Mystiker,
der Damaskus als Last empfand.
Neben dem Schrein ist eine Gebethalle.
Auf einer riesigen Leuchttafel
geben diodenrote Ziffern
die elektronisch exakte Zeit
für die fünf Gebete an.

Es gibt einen Gott dort, in Damaskus,
einen sehr grünen Gott. Falls er noch dort ist,
immer noch die Hand zum Gruß erhoben,
wird er nichts vergessen haben.

VERY GREEN

There's a god there, in Damascus;
a very green god
in a little display case
in a large museum.
Three thousand four hundred years ago
he was not forgetful
and never broke his promises.
Now he casts an amusing glance at the tourists.
The coat of gold that still remains
hinders him from folding his arms.
One hand is still raised in greeting;
the other's holding something that's disappeared.

At the edge of town
there's a very green cupola.
Under it Ibn el-Arabi
lies in his shrine. Under the cupola
beneath the broad vault
of a black green turban
he lies there, the mystic,
who felt Damascus to be a burden.
Next to the shrine is a prayer chamber.
Diode red numbers
on a giant luminous screen
give the electronically exact time
for the five prayers.

There's a god there in Damascus,
a very green god. In case he's still there
with his hand raised in greeting,
he will not have forgotten a thing.

GOLDEN, ISTANBUL

Erschrocken fällt der Mond zur Erde.
Wir wollen gehen, gehen nicht. Ziehend,
lähmend die Klarinette Barbaros Erköses.
Zuwachsende Kalligraphie. Sie aufreißen.

Sie waschen ohne Hände. Eine Biene
dringt da hinein. Kerbung, Kuhle.
Die Wunde glättest du. Du glänzt. Ich
werde sagen: Golden. Goldener Himmel

über dem *Sancelize Club*. Aufwachen und
sagen: Golden. Ich werde sagen: Nein,
nichts als das: Ich bin der Arkadaş,
der die gewundene Istiklal vergoldet

und das öläugige Horn – mit der Zeit,
gegen die Zeit, die nicht zählt, glückliche
Zeit, glückloser Klee auf dem Markt von Ortaköy,
wo wir den Tee aussitzen, die Augen nachziehen

über liebliche Hügel, Tulpen, Tauben, *Cöp,*
So tief hole ich mir die Stadt (übererklärt),
daß zuvor es keiner sieht. Eine Wasserstadt,
Wie geliebt wird, erfahren wir an ihr.

Nicht Verlangen zählt, das Gefühl, sagt
die Frau mit dem türkisch gerougten Bart.
Warum nur so besessen vom Schauen?
Hier werden Hamster auf Nippelringe dressiert.

Glaubst auch du: *Hamam tamam*?
Legst auch dich auf den heißesten Stein?
Doch ist der rote Vorhang nur in der Mitte
gerafft, Fumerie turque. *Burun Spray*:

GOLDEN, ISTANBUL

Startled, the moon falls to earth.
We want to go, not going. Enticing,
Immobilizing, the clarinet of Barbaros Erköse.
Overgrowths of calligraphy. Rip them open.

They wash without hands. A bee there
propelling inside. Crenellation. Coolness.
You smooth out the wound. You glisten. I
would say golden. Golden sky

over the *Sancelize Club*. Awaken and
say: golden. I would say: no,
nothing but that: I am the arcade
that gilds the sinuous Istiklal

and the buttery horn – in time,
counter the time, that doesn't count, lucky
time, luckless clover on the marketplace of Ortaköy,
where we sit out teatime, the eyes tracing

over lovely hills, tulips, doves, *Cöp*.
I seek the city at depths (over-explained),
no-one has seen before. A water city.
She reveals to us just how loved she is.

The feeling, not craving, counts, says
the woman with the rouged Turkish beard.
Why so possessed by looking?
Here even hamsters are dressed in nipple rings.

You also believe: *Hamam tamam?*
Do you, too, lie down on the hottest stone?
Yet, the red drape in the middle is only
tucked, *Fumerie turque. Burun Spray*:

Saft, der sich in Wangen verteilt, im Hirn.
Jetzt atmest du klar, siehtst endlich klar.
Bäuche hat es in Istanbul, Teekannen-Sirenen,
beschnittene Knaben im Ornat. Wasser aber

ist das Wichtigste. Unterströmungen
im Bosporus, Windstrudel von Beşiktaş
nach Üşküdar nach Eminönü. Mit reichlich
Sachen im Nachen. Fez et fesses.

Der Mond fällt erschrocken auf Büyük Ada.
Wir leben im Hôtel des Étrangers, mit Katzen,
einer Überdosis Eleganz. Die alte Dame im Luna Park
lehnt sich an die Tätowierung niederfallender Sterne.

Juice, that's splashed in cheeks, in the brain.
Now you breathe clearly, clear vision at last.
Bellies there are in Istanbul, teapot-sirens,
circumcised boys in priestly garb. Water, though,

is the most important. Undercurrents
in the Bosporus, whirlwind from Beşiktaş
to Üşküdar to Eminönü. With ample
provisions in the bark. *Fez et fesses.*

The startled moon falls on Büyük Ada.
We live in the *Hôtel des Étrangers*, with cats,
an overdose of elegance. The old lady in the Luna Park
props herself on the tattoos of downfallen stars.

HÔTEL DES ÉTRANGERS

Wir nahmen das Schiff nach Prinkipo, der größten
Prinzeninsel. Wir fühlten uns durchaus wohl.
Auf der Insel waren Griechen (assimiliert),
Armenier (assimiliert) und wir, andere Fremde.
Das Hotelpersonal sprach Türkisch, auch ein wenig
Französisch. So hielt sich unsere Traurigkeit
in Grenzen. Lieder und Photographien waren alles,
was wir mitnehmen konnten. Wir tauschten uns aus,
starrten auf das Wasser des Marmara-Meeres.
War unser Leben schon vorbei? Wir versuchten
wegzugehen mit Worten oder im Schlaf.
Manchmal tauchten wir nachts in immer kältere
Zonen der Sprachluft, die sich über Millionen
von Meilen erstreckten. Es war schwierig dann,
sich wieder an die Möwen, die Mimosen,
an Gesichter zu gewöhnen. Wir waren
wie bitter gewordene Feigen. Dunkelblau,
schrumpelig, an langen grauen Ästen.

HÔTEL DES ÉTRANGERS

We took the ship to Prinkipo, the largest
of the Princes Islands. We felt entirely at ease.
On the island were Greeks (assimilated),
Armenians (assimilated), and ourselves, other foreigners.
The hotel personnel spoke Turkish, also a little
French. So our sorrow was contained
within borders. Songs and photographs, all
that we could take with us, we exchanged with one another,
staring at the water of the Sea of Marmara.
Was our life already past? We attempted
to get away, with words or in sleep.
Sometimes we plunged at night
into ever colder zones of the lingual air
that extended for miles over millions.
Then it was difficult
to become accustomed again
to the seagulls, the mimosas,
and the faces. We were
like figs grown bitter. Dark blue,
wrinkled, on long grey branches.

AM HAFEN VON PAPHOS

Nach was riecht der Atem der Möwen?
Schalen, Tang?
Flachen Fischen mit brauner Haut?
Sie stehen, die Iris genadeltes Weiß,
in kleinen schlappen blauen Wellen
und starren ins Weite –

rosenplötzlich der Abend,
und Schlafland von Ost nach West.

Die alten Männer auf der Bank,
harte Knoten, lösen sich,
erinnern sich, wie sanft es war,
in ihr zu schwimmen.

Zum Hafen herab glänzt die Straße.
Ihr Rückgrat spult sich direkt aus der Sonne,
die untergeht, zischelnd (die Propheten, die Möwen).

Damals hielten wir Paphos für Gott.
Sein großer Zeh, hieß es, reiche an die Baumgrenze
des Toodos. Aber jetzt ist es eine nurtzlose Stadt

(nur manchmal noch erinnert
wie ein Palastfeuer).

THE HARBOR OF PAPHOS

What does the breath of seagulls smell like?
Shells, seaweed?
Flat fish with brown skin?
They stand, the iris pin-pointed white,
in little indolent blue waves
and stare out into the distance---

roseate-instantaneous the evening
and the Land of Nod from east to west.

The old men on the bench,
tough rustics, loosen up,
recalling how soft it was
to swim in her.

Down to the harbor the street's glistening,
its backbone uncoiling right out of the sun
that sets, hissing (the prophets, the seagulls).

At that time we looked on Paphos as God,
its big toe was said to stretch to the timberline
of Mt. Troodos. But now it's a useless city

(only sometimes still remembered
like a palace fire).

LAPITHOS

Wir saßen da mit den Palmen,
den Diwanen, Käfigen mit Kanarienvögeln.
Die Kinder lehnten die süßen Liköre ab.
So viele Dinge, die zu streicheln waren
und in den Gärten verschwanden.
Das Licht häutete behutsam das Haus,
bis es eine Fortsetzung des Meeres war.

LAPITHOS

We were sitting there with the palm trees,
the divans, cages with canary birds.
The children abstained from the sweet liqueur.
So many things there to caress
disappearing into the gardens.
The light carefully skinned the house
till it was an extension of the sea.

VON KARNAK
Für Uwe Timm

Die ältesten, von Karnak, sind die einfachsten.
Ein Kopf, breiter Panzer, stilisierte Flügel.
In Karneol, Elfenbein, Holz, Agat oder Gips.
Später ritzte man Wünsche in ihren Bauch
oder den Namen der Person, die ihn trug.
Noch später waren sie Ringe oder Siegel.

Am seltensten die Skarabäen des Herzens.
Die Ägypter glaubten, am Tor zur Unterwelt
werde das Herz eines jeden Menschen gewogen.
Es müsse leicht sein wie eine Feder.
Ein Herz-Skarabäus rettet ein schweres Herz.
Dein Herz ist leicht, federnd. Es glüht.

Die Gänge im Papier, dein Brutraum, könnten,
kleiner nur, auch Tunnel zu den Pharaonen sein.
Dort stehst du in großer Verbrüderung
mit Habicht und Springmaus, Kühle und Rausch.
Sie macht dich dort hungrig, wo sie am meisten
befriedigt. Am zitternden Nil. In der großen Menge

Sand der geschmeidige Skarabäus. So wie er sein Loch
in die Erde, so möchtest du der Liebsten ein Loch
ins Herz machen und dort deine Wörter ablegen:
Rebellion, Liebe, Wut, und da die Jahre vergehen,
Sehnsucht nach Rebellion, und da das Leben verworrener
wird, Klarheit. Die Klarheit des Himmels von Karnak.

FROM KARNAK

For Uwe Timm

The oldest, from Karnak, are the simplest.
A head, broad armour, stylized wings.
In carnelian, ivory, wood, agate or gypsum.
Later, wishes were etched in their belly
or the names of the person that bore them.
Later still, they were rings or seals.

Rarest of all, the scarabs of the heart.
The Egyptians believed that the heart of every person
would be swayed at the gate to the underworld.
It would have to be light as a feather.
A heart-scarabaeus saves a heavy heart.
Your heart is light, springy. It glows.

The pathways in the paper, your brooding place
but smaller, could be tunnels to the pharoahs, too.
There you stand in great fraternization
with hawk and jerboa, coolness and reverie.
She makes you hungry there where she satisfies you most.
At the trembling Nile. In the great multitude of sand

crawls the supple scarabaeus. Just as he hollows
the earth, so would you bore a hole in the heart
of the one you love most, and toss your words away
there: rebellion, love, rage, and when the years pass,
longing for rebellion, and when life grows more
muddled, clearness. The clearness of the sky over Karnak.

SANSIBAR

Stonetown

In Steinstadt
über den rostigen Wellblechdächern
verrostete Satellitenschüsseln,
in denen die Sonne, weich geschleudert,
                  grau verdampft.
An graue Mauern klatscht das Meer,
das nichts weiß als zu glitzern,
kleinste funkelnde Wellen. Blitzchen.
Krabben sind daher furchtsam hier.
Nur das Herz zerfällt.

Chumbe Island

Als der grüne Schirm des Sturms sich öffnet,
rauscht der Himmel herab.
Als der Schirm sich wieder schließt,
waren in der Luft 10 000 Termiten,
sind 20 000 Flügel zu Boden gefallen,
hat eine Armee von Eidechsen und Geckos
die flügellosen Leiber gefressen, knisternd.
Dann dampft die Erde stumm wie ein Kuß.
Unter der durchsichtigen Bauchhaut der Geckos
winzige Sprünge zuhauf noch, in engsten Falten.

Ras Nungwi

Regen. Plastikpalmen werden nicht gegossen.
Geschmack von Haaröl in der Mango,
von Staub im golddurchstochnem Nabel der
        Köchin.
Eine hellere Falte unter der Brust wie kühler
        Hermelin.
Wir lassen es uns zu gut gehen. Stellen
die Suche nach verschollenen Gefühlen ein.

ZANZIBAR

Stonetown

In Stonetown
above the rusty roofs of corrugated iron,
the sun, faintly pitched into
corroded satellite dishes, turns to
     grey vapor.
The sea, knowing nothing but how to glisten,
splashes against grey walls
the most delicate sparkling waves. Minute lightning flash.
The reason crabs are timid here.
Only the heart decays.

Chumbe Island

When the green umbrella of the storm opens up,
the sky roars down.
When the canopy closes again,
10,000 termites have filled the air,
20,000 wings falling to the ground,
an army of lizards and geckos
devouring the wingless bodies, crackling.
Then the earth dampens dumb as a kiss.
Under the diaphanous belly skin of the geckos
tiny squirmings still together in tightest folds.

Ras Nungwi

Rain. Plastic palms do not get drenched.
Taste of hair oil in the mango,
of dust in the cook's gold-pierced belly button.
A light crease below her breast like cool
  ermine.
We over indulge ourselves. Letting
the pursuit of forgotten feelings go.

Ein Regentropfen fällt ins Auge des Vogels.
Er singt. Pfeift wie ein Mensch. Rote Knopfaugen
vor milchgrünem Wasser, den weißen Linien
des Riffs, die am Horizont wandern,
sich treffen und meist nicht treffen.
Die Moräne, schüchtern, schaut dich nicht an,
                zupft am Felsen.

A raindrop falls into the bird's eye.
He sings. His whistling sounds human. Red button eyes
facing milky-green water, the white lines
of the reef, wandering into the horizon,
interweaving and for the most part, not.
The moraines, demurring, not returning your gaze,
tug at the rocks.

IV. KLEINER TOTENTANZ

>>*Wessen Name ausgesprochen wird,
der lebt.*<<

Inschrift auf der Statue eines Würfelhockers
in Priene, 2.Jh. v.Chr.

IV. LITTLE DANCE OF THE DEAD

"He, whose name is vocalized, lives."

Inscription on a block statue in Priene, 2nd century, B.C.

(Ritus)

Ich zerrieb den Zypressenzapfen
streng streng streng
auf deiner kleinen Brust
da warst du gestorben

(Ritus)

I rubbed the Cypress cone
hard hard hard
upon your small breast
for you were dead

AUF DEN BESTATTETEN

dieser Rumpf mit Stiel
diese Seele eine Fliege
dieses bißchen Fell
das einen aufregte
zwischen Beinen
und nach viel Nagen
der Zeit sterben geht
absichtsvoll
mit Gewebverfall
doch ein Geist
flackert doch
angespannter als im Leben
und ohne zu verstehen
genauso fassungslos so

TO THE BURIED

this torso with neck
this soul a fly
this bit of fur
that aroused one
between legs
and comes to die
on purpose
with decayed tissues
after time's incessant gnawing
yet a spirit
still flickers
more tensely than in life
and without understanding
so speechlessly precise

HINTÜBER

Das Leben beugt sich zurück im Tod,
Grimasse. Leder. Haare. Hintüber.
Grimassierer du. Blitz kracht
aus blauestem Himmel
ins Herz, wo nur Erscheinung ist,
nur arm verstücktes Gedächtnis.
Hintüber liegt's auf dem Rücken,
rote Adern unterm Kettenhemd,
die von Luft lebten, verglühendes
Männchen du, zappelnd,
ausgetickt: das dicke Ende.

So wie man nie ein Leben sah:
fertig, schmale Luft, unnahbar nah.
Die Augengebiete erloschen.

OVER BACKWARDS

Life bends back in death,
Grimace. Leather. Hair. Backwards.
Grimasseur you. Lightning flash cracks
from the bluest heaven
in the heart, where there's only apparition,
just poor segmented memory.
Lying over on his back,
red arteries that thrived on air
under the coat of mail, sputtering
manikin you, wriggling,
out for the count: the hell to pay.

A life such as one never saw:
finished, thin air, unapproachably close.
The eye-scapes extinguished.

KNOCHEN

ein kleines mittelmäßiges Nervenspiel
Saitenspiel Sehnenspiel
Bevor man stirbt wird man ganz Knochen
Knochen
Spür deine Knochen auf dem
Und das Wort Knochen
Und nicht im Mund nichts
im Bild, das die Augen denken:

Rauch, der fällt,
                fällt,
tropfend
        kein Widerhall –
        ein langer Schattenriegel im Osten

BONES

a small middling strain of nerves
strain of chords strain of tendons
Before dying one becomes entirely bones
bones
Feel your bones on . . . on . . .
And the word bones
And not in the mouth nothing
in the picture that the eyes think:

Smoke, that falls,
                    falls,
dripping
        no echo –
        a long shadow bolt in the east

DA IST DAS AUGE

Da ist das Auge
am Ende eines Knochenastes
und da, hinter der Stirn,
     noch Freude,
oft in der Schönheit gewesen zu sein;
   zu welchem Zwecke jetzt?
So viele Dinge, die in dir verschwanden
wie die Impfnarben an deinem Oberarm:
zwei geschlossene Augen, ein Augenpaar,
     das sehr langsam
in die übrige Haut hineinging.
Ich habe nichts verstanden.
Als mache verschwinden das Leben ganz.
Ein Schwerwerden.
Ein Müdigkeitsbuckel – aus Worten –
   ist das die Seele, die im Abflug
ihre Blicke zählt?

THERE IS THE EYE

There is the eye
at the end of a bony limb
and there, behind the brow,
                   still joy,
to have been in beauty often;
           to what purpose now?
so many things that have vanished into you,
like the vaccination marks on your upper arm;
two eyes shut tight, a pair of eyes,
                that very slowly
retracted into the rest of the skin.
I have understood nothing.
As if to disappear makes life whole.
A growing heaviness.
A knot of fatigue – out of words –
            is that the soul in flight
counting its glances?

HARZTOD
oder
VOM VERSCHWINDEN DER INSEKTEN

Jetzt, da ich tot bin, denk ich oft an dich.
In meinem goldenen Sarg, die Augennoppen
nachtaktiv. An dich Schmetterlingshafte,
andere Verschwundene, die aus dem Harz
blicken.
  Wie hat Kunst über Schönheit gesprochen,
wie die Natur? Natur in Form des Tanzes.
Um die tanzende Biene drängten wir uns
und wußten, wo die Blume ist, Geschmack
im Mund, schon grün, Begier.

Wir drängten uns um die tanzende Libelle,
die aufschlug unhörbar
      auf dem grauen Holz,
Gesirr, hypernervös. Die Wasserkäfer stiebten
ins Rohr, Wasserbahnen, die Wasser löschte,
kurze Zeit Strickmuster oder illuminierte Straßen,
auf denen die Kometin Libelle zog.

Helle des eng beringten Leibs, flirrend,
in Flügeln flirrend,
sirrend übers knisternde Holz.
Zu ihren Beinen der Schatten ihrer Beine,
Gestänge, das sich übers Wasser legte, Striche
geknickte im Bernstein. Ein letztes Vibrieren
hatte eine Schliere für die Zuckmücke gelassen,
die erstickte und mit dem Auge auf uns stürzt.

RESIN DEATH
or
FROM THE DISAPPEARENCE OF THE INSECTS

Now that I am dead, I think of you often.
In my gold sarcophagus, the eye naps
nocturnally active.
      Of you butterfly likeness,
of others disappeared, who peer out of the
resin.
       How has art spoken of beauty,
how has nature? Nature in form of the dance.
Round the dancing bumble-bee we were driven
Knowing where the flower was, taste
in the mouth, already green, desire.

We were driven round the dancing dragonfly,
that inaudibly hit
           on the grey wood,
Whirr, hyper-nervous. The water beetle flew off
in the reed, waterways that water liquidated,
criss-cross pattern for an instant, or illuminated street
where the comet dragonfly moves along its orbit.

Luminosity of the tight-ringed abdomen, flickering,
flickering in wings,
whirring above the rustling wood.
At their legs their legs' shadow,
small shafts, floating above the water, strokes
snapped off in the amber. A last vibration
has left a streak for the bloodworm,
that choked and collapses, staring at us.

JAHRESTAG

Da fand ich Geschmack an kurzen Worten
da übte ich mich in der Abwehr
des Andenkens
Messer

da färbte ich mich mit Altersfarben
dem Phosphor der Fischleber
schrieb jede Falte
voll und voll

ANNIVERSARY

This day I found good taste in terse words
This day I trained myself in the defense
of memory's
cutting edge

this day with fish liver phosophorus
I daubed myself in tints of age
filling each fold
with my writing

NACHT MIT DER HAND
Es ist, als schlafe er, wenn ich schlafe.
—Adonis, Gesänge für den Tod

Sie spitzt ihre Beine.
>>Ich habe wildes Fleisch im Nagelbett.<<
Nicht länger ist zu säumen.
Ich werf mich auf den Gliedergrund:
der grünste Stock
unter summenden Bäumen.

Der Schlaf hält still. Hat eine Maske.
Der Tod hält nicht still. Will
Knochen vom Rücken pflücken.
Sie scheucht ihn ins Gezweig,
und doch und noch
sein Summen, sein Rascheln.

NIGHT WITH THE HAND

It is, as if it were sleeping, when I sleep.
—Adonis, *Songs for Death*

She points her legs.
"In the nail-bed I have wild flesh."
No longer time to hesitate.
I throw myself aground:
the greenest rod
Under buzzing trees.

Sleep stops still. Wears a mask.
Death does not stop still. Wants
to pluck bones from the back.
She shoos him into the branches,
and yet and yet
his buzzing, his rustling.

TOTE FRAUEN LIEBEN

Tote Frauen sind fremde Frauen,
die wir nicht mehr berühren können.
Haben wir sie je berührt? Das Auge perlt.
Schon immer hat der Schimmer dieser Frauen
Berührungen unmöglich gemacht. Tränen
verzittern nun die Bilder der Erinnerung.
Die Frauen liegen kalt mit dem Gesicht im Laub.

Von toten Frauen Fotos: Am Strand, auf Bäumen,
im Bett. Zerknittert, von Lichtflecken ramponiert.
Schaut nicht so tot. Lächelt nicht so erfroren.
Am felsigen Sockel machen Wellen
hartnäckig aus Marmor Milch.
Aus in Porzellanhaut eingelassenen Adern
ein Gespinst Unsterblichkeit.

Ihr toten Frauen seid sehr schön.
Es läßt sich nicht wegtauchen unter dem Radar
der Liebe. Wir messen die Haut, den Spann,
die Linie – langsam – des Halses,
die unermeßliche Fläche vom Nacken zum Rist,
mit einer Bucht plötzlich in der Mitte des Weges,
wir suchen, wir messen, bis eine Stelle

Lust verspricht, eine Himmelswölbung,
die bebt. Erdbebengleich: >>Und denkt daran,
wie eine Frau alle Arten Tod in sich
aufnehmen kann und doch weiter lebt.<<
Als gebe Tiefe Antwort. Sie gibt sie nicht.
Es zählt der nicht berührbare Schimmer,
ganz oben auf der Haut. Jener Glanz.

DEAD WOMEN LOVE

Dead women are foreign women,
whom we cannot touch anymore.
Have we touched them ever? The eye glistens.
All along, the shimmer of these women
has made contact impossible. Tears
blur the images of memory now.
The women lie cold face down in the leaves.

From dead women photos: on the beach, in trees,
in the bed. Crumpled, marred by faded spots.
Don't look so dead. Don't smile so frost-bitten.
On the rocky plinth waves make
obdurate milk out of marble.
Out of veins set in porcelain skin
a tissue of eternity.

You dead women are very lovely.
There is no ducking under the radar
of love. We measure the skin, the instep,
the curvature – slowly – of the neck,
the immeasurable surface from the nape to the arch,
with an inlet suddenly in the middle of the course,
we search, we measure, till a place

promises pleasure, a vault of heaven,
that quakes. Earthquake-like: "And remember,
how a woman can absorb every kind of death
in herself and still live on."
As were profound answer given. She gives it not.
What counts is the shimmer that cannot be touched
on skin's outer surface. That sheen.

Tote Frauen sind grausam. In diesem Haus
Sind einzig anwesend die Abwesenden,
und die Erinnerung, das sind die Geliebten,
welche unerreichbar bleiben, die wir hatten
und nicht mehr haben, und jene, die wir niemals
hatten. Die uns ins Licht tauchten. Die sagten:
Du wirst nichts erleben und nur Abschied nehmen.

Dead women are cruel. In this house
the absent are singularly present,
and the memory, those are the sweethearts,
who remain out of reach, whom we had
and have no more, and those we never
had. Who dipped us into the light. Who said:
You will live to see nothing and only bid farewell.

CREDO

Und die Nächte, waren sie nicht lang?
Dehnten sie sich nicht ringsum in die
von Sonne verprügelte Steppe? Ich kaufte
Salzbarren, weiß wie Schneezikaden,
Gebetsknochen. So gerüstet reisten wir.

Die Sternengreise über uns, fünfmal
schwerer als die Sonne, stäubten.
Wir rissen uns am Kameldorn wund und
glaubten an kommende Quellgebiete,
bis wie von Nichts das Nichts sich öffnete.

CREDO

And the nights, were they not long?
Did they not stretch out all around
the sun-scourged steppes? I bought
bars of salt, white like snow cicadas,
prayer bones. Thus armed did we journey.

The greybeard stars above us, five times
heavier than the sun, emitted dust.
We pricked ourselves raw on camel's thorn and
believed headwaters were coming, until
– as if out of Nothing – Nothingness revealed itself.

JUGEND UND ALTER DES FORSCHERS

Tod, der alles nimmt, wird dir
nicht den Gesang nehmen.
—*Kallimachos (310–240 v.Chr.)*

Als er jung war,
nutzte er das Hirn für Inszenierungen.
Kalibrierte den Versuch, Sehen zu sehen.

Sein Blick
kehrte sich von den Sternen ab,
um in das Auge selbst zu sehen.

In seine Bibliothek
wurden Schüsseln voll Augäpfel getragen.
Er zerlegte sie mit dem Skalpell.

Wie Lasuren in der Malerei
lagen die Membrane übereinander.
Schicht auf Schicht legte er sie frei,

schälte die Retina ab,
wußte plötzlich, er war schon alt:
Augenglück macht Augen stark.

Sang das. Den scharfen Lobpreis
auf das Glück, daß er in Blicken,
nicht in Worten war.

YOUTH AND OLD AGE OF THE RESEARCHER

Death, he taketh all away,
But song he cannot take.
—*Callimachus (310-240 B.C.)*

When he was young,
he used his brain for *mise-en-scènes*.
Calibrating the attempt to see seeing.

His glance
he turned away from the stars,
to peer into the eye itself.

In his library
tureens were carried full of eyeballs.
He dissected them with the scalpel.

Like lazuli in painting
the membranes lay on top of each other.
Layer after layer he peeled their veils free,

unshelling the retina,
Suddenly knowing he was already old:
Auspicious sight makes eyes strong.

Sang that. The keen acclaim
for the good fortune that was his in looks,
not words.

BLEIBT IRIS

während das Licht aus den Augen geht,
weg geht, fort geht, bleibt
die Farbe der Iris, bleibt
die wunde Haut, bleibt
der rote Lack auf den Fingernägeln,
die einer Hand gehören,
die neben einer Brust liegt,
die Gänsehaut hat und scharf
wächst und mündet
in weiße Nervennetze,
ich mag sie nicht, ich
mag dich nicht, ich
schau dir meine Leiche

STAY IRIS

whereas the light in the eyes goes out,
departs, disappears, the color of iris
remains, the chapped skin remains,
the red polish on the fingernails
that belong to a hand
lying next to a breast
that has goosebumps
and grows
prickly, ending
in white bundles of nerves,
I don't like them, I
don't like you, I show
you my corpse.

(Ritus)

bevor du aus der Welt gehst
steh auf verlasse noch einmal das Bett
und gehe von Zimmer zu Zimmer
hefte in jedem Zimmer die Augen
auf Türen und Fenster
Tische und Ecken
die pudernde Kalkschicht der Wände
dann leg dich wieder hin
dein Terrain wird bleiben

(Ritus)

before you step out of the world
stand up leave your bed one more time
and go from room to room
fix your eyes in every one
on doors and windows
tables and corners
the walls' powdery layer of chalk
then lay yourself down
your terrain will endure

ANNOTATIONS

"In Writing": *"Der Schmetterling als Gespenst der Raupe"* ("The butterfly as phantom of the caterpillar") is a notation in Elias Canetti's *Totenbuch* (Book of the Dead), which I employ here with slight modification.

The section *Some Picture Poems* is concerned with paintings that I've discovered by Joachim Patinir, a Flemish painter, who died in Antwerp in 1524. Albrecht Dürer, who accepted Patinir's invitation to attend his second wedding, depicts him in his journal as a "good landscape painter". In 2007, the Prado museum in Madrid organized the very first exhibit of Patinir, gathering together the 28 paintings that can unequivocally be attributed to him. The Patinir-cycle of poems arose from visits to this exhibit in the Prado.

Kerkennah is the name of one of the group of flat islands situated in front of the Tunisian port city of Sfax and already colonized in ancient times by the Romans.

Fischitani is a colloquial Moroccan Arabic expression meaning: "Is that all? Don't you have anything else?"

Golden, Istanbul: *cöp* is the Turkish word for garbage, *burun spray* for nasal spray. Besiktas, Üşküdar and Eminönü are names of municipal districts in Istanbul. Büyük Ada (Great Island) is the name of the largest Prince Island, which the Greeks called "Prinkipo". The trip from Istanbul to Büyük Ada takes but an hour.

The "Hôtel des Étrangers" in the 1920s and 1930s was one of the large hotels on the island of Prinkipo (Büyükada), which accepted many exiles.

Lapithos is the Greek name of a village in northern Cypress, not far from Kyrenia.

Joachim Sartorius, 2013

Joachim Sartorius was born in Fürth, Bavaria in 1946 and grew up in Tunis. He studied law and political science in Munich, London, and Paris, and served as a diplomat in New York, Istanbul, and Nicosia until 1986. After holding various positions in the field of international cultural policy, he was Director General of the Berlin Festivals from 2000 to 2011.

He has published nine volumes of poetry, available in translation in twelve foreign languages, including *Ice Memory, Selected Poems* (Carcanet, 2013). He has also published a book of essays *The Inside of Ships* (Dumont, 2006), an essay in book form *Poetry and Time* (Seagull Press, 2019), and two travelogues: *The Princes Islands* (Haus Publishing, 2009) and *The Geckos of Bellapais* (Haus Publishing, 2014).

His publishing projects include translations of the collected works of both Malcolm Lowry and William Carlos Williams; as well as works by Wallace Stevens, John Ashbery, and Allen Curnow, among others. Sartoris has collaborated on books with artists James Lee Byars, Nan Goldin, and Max Neumann; and edited the following international poetry anthologies: *Atlas of New Poetry* (Rowohlt Verlag,1995), *Minima Poetica* (Kiepenheuer & Witsch, 1999), *Alexandria Fata Morgana* (DVA, 2002), *Never a Breathing Spell: Handbook of Political Verse in the 20th Century* (Kiepenheuer & Witsch, 2014).

Scott J. Thompson is former editor-in-chief of the online Walter Benjamin Research Syndicate (1996-2016). He studied German in Freiburg im Breisgau in the 1970s, continuing his studies at the University of Wisconsin–Madison, and obtaining an M.A. in German at San Francisco State University. He has published translations in *The New German Critique, Leftcurve, The Journal of Cognitive Liberties,* and *Cabinet.* His translation of alchemical stories by Johann Wolfgang von Goethe, *Tales for Transformation*, was published by City Lights Books in 1987.

THE DIVERS COLLECTION

Number 1
Hôtel des Étrangers, poems by **Joachim Sartorius** translated from German to English by **Scott J. Thompson**

Number 2
Inside the Studio, a memoir by **Mary Julia Klimenko**

Number 3
XISLE, a novel by **Tamsin Spencer Smith**

Made in the USA
Monee, IL
28 December 2020

55679304R00069